OREGON TRAIL

Virginia Loh-Hagan

45TH PARALLEL PRESS

Published in the United States of America by Cherry Lake Publishing Group
Ann Arbor, Michigan
www.cherrylakepublishing.com

Reading Adviser: Marla Conn, MS, Ed., Literacy specialist, Read-Ability, Inc.
Book Designer: Melinda Millward

Photo Credits: © Keith Lance/iStock.com, front cover, 1; © Victorian Traditions/Shutterstock.com, 4;
© Steve Lagreca/Shutterstock.com, 6; © v.gi/Shutterstock.com, 8; © Tony Craddock/Adobe Stock,
10, back cover; © Library of Congress, LC-DIG-highsm-38249, 12; © Soulart/Shutterstock.com, 14;
©bauhaus1000/iStock.com, 16, 24, 26; © Krasnova Ekaterina/Shutterstock.com, 19; © James Gabbert/
Shutterstock.com, 20; © Russ Heinl/Shutterstock.com, 22; © bauhaus1000/iStock.com, 26; © Jon
Bilous/Shutterstock.com, 28

Graphic Element Credits: © Milos Djapovic/Shutterstock.com, back cover, front cover; © cajoer/
Shutterstock.com, back cover, front cover, multiple interior pages; © GUSAK OLENA/Shutterstock.com,
back cover, multiple interior pages; © Miloje/Shutterstock.com, front cover; © Rtstudio/Shutterstock.
com, multiple interior pages; © Konstantin Nikiteev/Dreamstime.com, 29

Library of Congress Cataloging-in-Publication Data

Names: Loh-Hagan, Virginia, author.
Title: Oregon Trail / by Virginia Loh-Hagan.
Description: Ann Arbor, Michigan : Cherry Lake Publishing, [2021] | Series: Surviving history | Includes
    index.
Identifiers: LCCN 2020030328 (print) | LCCN 2020030329 (ebook) | ISBN 9781534180284 (hardcover) |
    ISBN 9781534181991 (paperback) | ISBN 9781534181298 (pdf) | ISBN 9781534183001 (ebook)
Subjects: LCSH: Oregon National Historic Trail—History—Juvenile literature. | Pioneers—Oregon National
    Historic Trail—History—19th century—Juvenile literature. | Pioneers—Oregon National Historic Trail—Social
    life and customs—19th century—Juvenile literature. | Frontier and pioneer life—Oregon National Historic
    Trail—Juvenile literature. | Overland journeys to the Pacific—Juvenile literature.
Classification: LCC F597 .L695 2021 (print) | LCC F597 (ebook) | DDC 978/.02—dc23
LC record available at https://lccn.loc.gov/2020030328
LC ebook record available at https://lccn.loc.gov/2020030329

Cherry Lake Publishing Group would like to acknowledge the work of the Partnership for 21st Century
Learning, a Network of Battelle for Kids. Please visit http://www.battelleforkids.org/networks/p21
for more information.

Printed in the United States of America
Corporate Graphics

TABLE OF CONTENTS

INTRODUCTION

Many Americans saw the West as the future. They wanted new lives.

In 1803, President Thomas Jefferson bought land from the French. This deal was called the Louisiana Purchase. It doubled the size of the United States. In 1862, President Abraham Lincoln signed the **Homestead** Act. Homesteads are homes and the land around them. The U.S. government gave free land to farmers. Farmers had to live on the land for 5 years. They had to improve the land. These events inspired people to travel west. People wanted land. They built new cities.

Americans had already started leaving their homes in 1840. From then until 1870, they headed west from the East Coast. This was called Westward **Expansion**. Expansion means a growth. These Americans traveled along the Oregon Trail. The Oregon Trail was a major **route**. Routes are paths.

In 1978, the U.S. government officially named the trail the Oregon National Historic Trail. Only 300 miles (483 kilometers) of the original trail is left.

The Oregon Trail began in Independence, Missouri. It ended in Oregon City, Oregon. The Oregon Trail travelers were **pioneers**. Pioneers are the first people to explore or settle an area. In 1843, about 1,000 people traveled on the Oregon Trail.

The Oregon Trail was known as this nation's "longest graveyard." Pioneers faced many dangers. About 1 in 10 pioneers died. There were about 10 deaths per mile.

The Oregon Trail route ended when railroads were built. This happened in the late 1800s. Trains were easier, faster, and safer than wagons.

GROUP OR ALONE?

Travel guidebooks had important information and tips for pioneers. The books described road conditions. They listed camping areas.

To be successful, pioneers needed to be organized. They planned meals. They packed. They camped. They secured animals. They made repairs.

Most pioneers traveled in groups. They banded together. They helped each other. They protected each other. Families traveled together. People from the same hometown traveled together. Friends traveled together.

Some people joined **companies**. Companies are professional groups. They were the most organized. They had trail guides. These companies had leaders. They had schedules. They had rules. They punished people for breaking rules.

The Donner Party had about 87 pioneers. They took a shortcut. They got trapped in the mountains. Some people froze to death. Some died of hunger. The survivors ate the dead bodies.

QUESTION 1

Would you travel by yourself or with others?

A You traveled with a company. You had an expert lead you on the trail. You had guards to keep you safe. You had to listen to a leader. You did what you were told. You shared resources. You helped the group.

B You traveled with your family. You had what you brought with you. You had what you could buy along the way. You could only rely on each other.

C You traveled alone. You could do whatever you wanted. You had a lot of freedom. But you had to figure things out by yourself. You had to protect yourself.

The heavy traffic turned the land into dust. Dust got everywhere.

SURVIVOR BIOGRAPHY

Narcissa Prentiss Whitman lived from 1808 to 1847. She was born in New York. Whitman and her husband were missionaries. Missionaries are people sent to promote religion. In 1836, the Whitmans traveled west. They took a small group. They started in St. Louis, Missouri. They headed to Walla Walla Valley in Oregon. (Today, it's in Washington.) The Whitmans traveled by sleigh. They traveled by boat. They traveled by wagon. They traveled by horseback. They traveled by foot. They went farther west than any other Americans before them. At 28 years old, Whitman became one of the first white women to cross the Rocky Mountains. She kept a journal. She also wrote letters home. Her letters were published in East Coast newspapers. She inspired people to travel west.

SPRING OR FALL?

Landmarks were useful for pioneers on the trail.
An important landmark called Devil's Gate was
located in the mountains of Wyoming.

Pioneers had to travel about 2,000 miles (3,219 km). The Oregon Trail was a hard trip. Pioneers traveled through mountains. They traveled on rough roads. They traveled through rivers. They traveled in bad weather.

They traveled about 15 to 20 miles (24 to 32 km) a day. Most pioneers traveled west around April 15. This meant they'd be on the West Coast by September. An ideal trip took 4 to 5 months.

Timing was important. This was because of weather. Weather could cause a lot of problems. April and May could be rainy and wet. Summers could be dry and hot. Dust was a big problem in hot months. Winters were cold and harsh.

QUESTION 2

When would you start traveling on the Oregon Trail?

A You set off in the spring. Grass grows in the spring. This meant animals could eat along the way. You had a good chance of crossing the Oregon mountains before heavy snows started.

B You set off in the summer. You'd have to deal with strong **prairie** thunderstorms. Prairies are open grasslands. These storms included heavy rains. They included hail. They included high winds.

C You set off in the fall. You'd be traveling during the winter months. You could get **frostbite**. Frostbite is the freezing of the skin. You could also freeze to death.

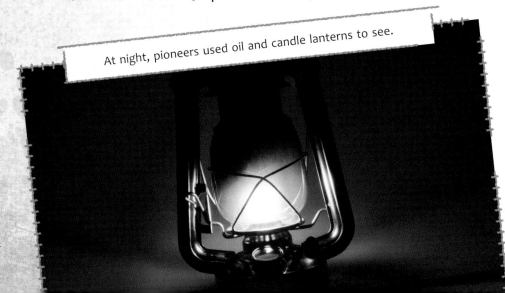

At night, pioneers used oil and candle lanterns to see.

SURVIVAL BY THE NUMBERS

- About 20,000 to 30,000 pioneers died of **cholera** and other sicknesses. Cholera makes people throw up.
- Between 1840 and 1860, about 300 pioneers drowned while trying to cross rivers.
- Around 80,000 of the 400,000 pioneers ended their journey in Oregon's Willamette Valley.
- About 250,000 pioneers traveled the California Trail. Most were looking for gold.
- Fort Laramie is in Wyoming. It became known as Camp Sacrifice. Pioneers dumped their trash and extra things there. In 1849, they dumped 20,000 pounds (9,072 kilograms) of bacon outside of Fort Laramie's walls.
- Supplies in wagons had to weigh under 2,000 pounds (907 kg). About 1,600 pounds (726 kg) would be food.
- It cost about $600 to get a wagon, oxen, and basic supplies. That's about $15,000 today!
- Only 1 of every 250 pioneers kept a written record. Many were lost or destroyed.

WAGON OR WALK?

People followed other wagons. This was called a wagon train.

Most pioneers traveled by covered wagons. These wagons looked like boats going over the rolling lands of the West. That's why they were called prairie **schooners**. Schooners are boats.

The wagons were made of wood. They had iron around the wheels. They were about 10 feet (3 meters) long. They were about 4 feet (1.2 m) wide. They were pulled by strong animals. Most pioneers used mules or oxen. Mules and oxen could work a long time. They were less likely to be stolen than horses.

Pioneers packed everything they could in their wagons. Most times, pioneers walked alongside the wagons. This let the wagons carry more things. Plus, riding in wagons was bumpy. It was not comfortable.

QUESTION 3

How did you travel?

A You traveled with a wagon. You carried supplies in your wagon. You hid underneath your wagon during storms. You slept in your wagon for safety. You were covered from the sun.

B You traveled on horseback. You could travel faster than wagons. But you had limited supplies. You weren't protected from the weather. Also, horses won't eat the prairie grasses. You had to carry grain to feed your horse.

C You walked. You only took what you could carry. You put your things in a handcart. You pushed the cart. Or you put your things in a backpack. You ran out of food.

Wagons had to be light enough to pull.

HEALTHY OR SICK?

If someone died while traveling, they were buried on the trail.
This was so wild animals wouldn't eat their bodies.

Pioneers were tired. They had bad diets. They drank dirty water. They didn't bathe. They didn't clean their clothes. They left garbage everywhere. They lived in **unsanitary** conditions. Unsanitary means dirty.

Many pioneers got sick. They lived close together. This quickly spread sickness. Sickness was the biggest cause of death.

Some pioneers died of food poisoning. Some died from the flu. Some died from measles. Some died from mumps.

Most pioneers died of cholera. It makes people poop. It's painful. People became **dehydrated**. Dehydrated means not having enough water in your body. People with cholera could die within hours.

There were very few doctors on the Oregon Trail. Pioneers didn't have the right medicine.

QUESTION 4

How would you have accessed safe drinking water?

A You had a wagon. This meant you could carry a water **keg**. Kegs are containers. You collected fresh water. You boiled it. You stored it in the kegs. You always had safe water with you.

B You didn't have a wagon. You drank from springs and rivers along the way. You knew how to clean the water. You used cornmeal to filter out the sand and other bits.

C You didn't have a wagon. You also didn't know how to clean water. You drank water wherever you could.

Most of the Oregon Trail was close to water sources. But there were areas that were dry.

SURVIVAL TOOLS

Many pioneer women packed Dutch ovens in their wagons. Dutch ovens are large cast-iron cooking pots. They have lids. Their lids fit tightly around the top. Dutch ovens last a long time. They're hard to chip, crack, or break. They hold a lot of heat. They can be used in high heat. They can be placed directly over a fire. They can also be buried. Hot coals are placed on the lid. This turns Dutch ovens into baking ovens. Pioneer women made all kinds of things with Dutch ovens. They made stews and soups. They made breads. They could bake food. They could roast food. They could deep-fry food. They could steam food. They even used the lids as skillets. But Dutch ovens are heavy. They weigh about 30 pounds (14 kg). They require a lot of wood to heat up. So, if needed, they were often left behind on the trail.

TO CROSS OR NOT TO CROSS?

Some pioneers died from being stuck
in cold river water for too long.

The second cause of death on the Oregon Trail was **accidents**. Accidents are unplanned events that cause damage or harm. Wagon accidents were common. Many children fell under the wheels of a moving wagon. They'd get crushed. Shooting accidents were also common. Many pioneers had guns. Most didn't know how to use them. They'd accidentally shoot themselves or each other.

Crossing rivers caused the most accidents. This was the most dangerous thing pioneers had to do. Rivers flooded. People and animals drowned in them. Wagon wheels could be damaged by rocks. They could get stuck in the muddy bottom.

QUESTION 5

How would you handle a river crossing?

A Pioneers before you had set up **ferries** and bridges. Ferries are boats that carry people and things across water. You crossed using the ferries. You had the money to pay to use them.

B You turned your wagon into a boat. You tried to lead your wagons and animals across rivers. You tried to avoid fast waves and floods.

C You tried to cross the river on your own. But you couldn't swim. You tried to find another route. This made your trip longer.

Ferry owners made a lot of money. They charged for each animal. They charged for each wagon.

SURVIVAL TIPS

Follow these tips to survive a river crossing:

- Climb a tree. Or get to higher ground. Check for obstacles in the river. Look for bridges. Look for wide areas where the river is slower and shallower.
- Throw a stick in the water. Walk alongside it. If the stick moves faster than you, the river is too fast. Avoid crossing.
- Don't cross upstream of fallen trees. Trees can hold you underwater.
- Wait 24 hours after a storm.
- Wear water shoes. Avoid slipping.
- Use a stick or pole as a guide. Face upstream. Walk a diagonal path. Walk against the current. Currents are waves.
- Cross with more people. Groups are more stable. Put hands on each other's shoulders. Have the strongest people in the front and back of the line.
- Move with purpose. Make sure each step is secure.

SURVIVAL RESULTS

Some parts of the trail are still visible today.

Would you have survived?

Find out! Add up your answers to the chapter questions. Did you have more **A**s, **B**s, or **C**s?

- If you had more **A**s, then you're a survivor! Congrats!

- If you had more **B**s, then you're on the edge. With some luck, you might have just made it.

- If you had more **C**s, then you wouldn't have survived.

Are you happy with your results? Did you have a tie?

Sometimes fate is already decided for us. Follow the link below to our webpage. Scroll until you find the series name *Surviving History*. Click download. Print out the template. Follow the directions to create your own paper die. Read the book again. Roll the die to find your new answers. Did your fate change?

https://cherrylakepublishing.com/teaching_guides

DIGGING DEEPER: DID YOU KNOW...?

The Oregon Trail was exciting and dangerous. It led to a new life for many Americans. But many lives were lost. Surviving history involves many different factors. Dig deeper. Consider some of the facts below.

QUESTION 1:

Would you travel alone or with others?

- Companies were within a day away from one another.
- Many companies and families took a milk cow.
- When parents died, children were left alone. Some were adopted by other pioneers.

QUESTION 2:

When would you start traveling on the Oregon Trail?

- Pioneers who left in the spring reached the desert in the summer.
- Storms caused delays. Delays meant pioneers would have to travel in the winter.
- Food is scarce in the winter. Pioneers die from hunger.

QUESTION 3:

How did you travel?

- Wagons were sometimes brightly painted. Pioneers did this to show they were traveling in a group.
- Men on horseback would ride ahead. They cleared a path.
- As pioneers walked, dust got into their eyes. It got into their lungs.

QUESTION 4:

How would you have accessed safe drinking water?

- Pioneers could not carry enough water to make the whole trip. They had to collect water along the way.
- Human and animal waste, garbage, and dead animal bodies were close to water. This poisoned the water.
- The worst cholera outbreaks occurred on the Oregon Trail in 1849, 1850, and 1852.

QUESTION 5:

How would you handle a river crossing?

- Native Americans helped ferry pioneers across rivers in their canoes.
- Some pioneers made simple rafts by tying logs together.
- Animals panic in water. They could hurt their owners.

GLOSSARY

accidents (AK-sih-dehnts) unplanned events that cause damage or harm

cholera (KAH-lur-uh) a sickness that makes people throw up and poop

companies (KUHM-puh-neez) professional groups

dehydrated (dee-HYE-dray-tid) lacking water in your body

expansion (ik-SPAN-shuhn) growth

ferries (FER-eez) floating vehicles that deliver people and things across water

frostbite (FRAWST-bite) the freezing of the skin

homestead (HOME-sted) homes and the land around them

keg (KEG) large container

pioneers (pye-uh-NEERZ) the first people to explore or settle an area

prairie (PRAIR-ee) open grasslands

route (ROOT) path

schooners (SKOO-nurz) boats

unsanitary (un-SAN-ih-ter-ee) dirty

LEARN MORE!

- Loh-Hagan, Virginia. *Heading West: Oregon Trail and Westward Expansion.* Ann Arbor, MI: Cherry Lake Publishing, 2019.
- Marciniak, Kristin. *The Oregon Trail and Westward Expansion.* Ann Arbor, MI: Cherry Lake Publishing, 2014.
- Russo, Kristin J. *Viewpoints on the Oregon Trail and Westward Expansion.* Ann Arbor, MI: Cherry Lake Publishing, 2019.

INDEX

ABOUT THE AUTHOR

Dr. Virginia Loh-Hagan is an author, university professor, and former classroom teacher. She's been to Oregon several times. Her husband went to the University of Oregon. She lives in San Diego with her very tall husband and very naughty dogs. To learn more about her, visit www.virginialoh.com.